Copyright © 2024 by Emma Walker.

All rights reserved. No part of this book may be used or reproduced in any form whatsoever without written permission except in the case of brief quotations in critical articles or reviews.

ISBN - Paperback: 978-1-06702-490-1

This book is dedicated to the loss
of someone so close to my heart,
they have half of it with them

Emma Walker

Words, part 1

I have encountered a human,

they opened their mouth.

Their lips moved.

The venom strikes,

not again I think,

but here we are again,

Pulse increases,

Mind racing,

Body wants to run away,

far away,

where people cannot say the "wrong thing".

Grief between the lines

Do I speak,

will the words come out?

will they understand.

Is it me,

I over think,

I take everything the wrong way,

I focus on the details,

only the ones that hurt.

Thats where I am at,

wary of people,

their words,

their actions.

Wary, full stop.

Emma Walker

Words, part 2.

The relief washes over,

Their words can feel like home.

They may be a stranger,

or they may be a loved one.

Either can make a dent in the trajectory of your day.

They open their mouth,

words of comfort fall out.

Your ear perks,

you tear down part of your wall,

you lean in to seek comfort in the safety of their words.

Grief between the lines

Days like these

The pain, long and winding more than any country road, more turbulent than a rogue wave engulfing a dinghy in high seas.

Deep breaths, mindfulness, and fresh air pale in comparison to the magnitude of the heartache.

Emma Walker

Sunrise

Sleep is not restful when you keep waking up to your worst nightmare.

Sunrise doesn't look so pretty when you're not sharing it with your loved one.

Bird song doesn't sound the same anymore, instead of the sound of nature, now it's like an alarm clock, reminding you to wake up and endure another day. on earth without your precious loved one.

Grief between the lines

Self-care

When your grieving, people harp on about this foreign concept called self-care.

How does one look at a warm bathtub the same when their entire existence has been shaken to its core.

How is a hot drink really meant to be savoured when all you see it as now is hot liquid in a cup that might provide some energy at best.

Go outside for a walk they say, so you take your grief for a walk. It may help to ease the suffocating feelings, or you may spot triggers while out, which try to drop you to your knees.

They make you want to bury your head in the leaves, the grass, the sand, whichever will cover your tear-streaked face.

Emma Walker

The aftermath

The wave crashes and tumbles you
through its turbulent waters, like
a delicate woollen knit enduring a
heavy-duty washing machine cycle.
You gasp for air as you are plunged
deeper into the depths of the
rolling wave.

When the wave has hit the shore,
you slowly and gingerly rise to the
surface, struggling for air, for a
break between sets.

Treading water in the shallows
wondering when the next wave will
crash over you, drowning you,
pushing you further into the depths
of despair.

Grief between the lines

Clouds

The clouds have moved in,

there is no running,

no hiding,

no seeking solace

They are coming,

keep yourself safe,

for they do not take mercy on your tender heart.

They come no matter what. They do not answer to a schedule or give notice, they just come.

Emma Walker

Alien

Am I green and slimy,

do I speak an undiscovered language,

or am I diseased.

For it feels I may belong on a different planet, one where it feels I will be seen.

I know you think of me or at least that is what you said, many moons ago, exactly when I just do not know.

When I say I need you, it does not mean in the flesh, there are other ways to stay near, to remind me you are there.

You know how to contact me in my UFO. We are worlds apart, but how about trying to make a start. Show me we are closer than I think, even in a symbol or a wink.

Grief between the lines

Alien cont'd ...

If you feel scared of what to say,
the silence is deafening, so please
be brave and do not shy away.

I know I am an alien, there are
reminders every day. I have pain
that cannot be silenced but please
hold my hand anyway.

Emma Walker

Walls

To navigate the loneliness

I have built a lot of walls.

These walls were built alone,

and that is how you will find me.

Scared to let people in,

for I am feeling fragile,

and it is hard to crack a smile.

So, if you ask to see me,

it could take me a while.

Grief between the lines

Isolation

I look for quiet places,

places I can cry.

Places free of triggers, they are hard to find.

Countless tears in public, streaming as I walk.

Too sad to talk to strangers but too stubborn to walk away.

I want to exist in society, but I do not know what to say.

Emma Walker

My constant

As I wake in the morning, I think of you. As I try to figure out how to fill my day without you in it, I think of you.

As I drive my car, I think of you. In the bathtub, I think of you.

Listening to music, I think of you. Drinking coffee, I think of you.

While I am crying, I am thinking of you, crying because your gone.

Every moment, of every day, I think you.

Grief between the lines

Friends

Selfless spirits,

strong minds,

very hard to find.

Some may surprise you,

they never shy away,

while others leave you wanting

every single day.

When you find the constants,

you want to hold them close.

They are your safe people,

those you love the most.

Emma Walker

Flowers

Please do not send me flowers,

their beauty I cannot see.

My glass is almost empty,

I cannot picture it as full.

Please do not expect me to be grateful.

as it forces me to lie.

How can I be grateful?

when my loved one did not survive.

So please do not send me flowers,

I do not want them on my mind.

Grief between the lines

Self-care revisited

In the midst of emotion, you run the bath for comfort.

Disappointed with what you find.

It is like a teaspoon of tepid water when you crave a gallon of tea.

Walking is like admission to a revolving hamster wheel, it makes you feel like you could keep walking, trying to escape the reality that you never get to hold them again.

A massage is distracting for those moments on the table. The minute that pressure eases, your pain rushes back in like a stampede of spooked elephants.

Emma Walker

Nothing really matters

You don't care for nonsense.

You don't care for material things,

nor do you care

for the most mundane of things.

The things that used to matter,
won't ever make the grade. Anything
superficial is banished out of
sight.

Now you know what really matters,

and that is wishing you were alive.

Grief between the lines

Weather

Some days a crack of light will glimpse through the shadows.

Other days all that is fore casted is a category graded storm.

Do not beat yourself up in the stormy weather, it will take longer to get dry.

Instead wrap yourself up with whatever may bring you a small slice of peace.

If all you do on the days where there is a tiny clearing inn the weather is fight like anything to keep it that way, then that is more than enough, more than anyone could expect of you.

Keep on weathering, there will come a time where you can put away a couple of umbrellas amongst the army that is trying to keep you safe in the storm.

Emma Walker

Anger

Grief and all its twists and turns. There are not enough plates in a department store to smash that would release this level of pain. Its immense and unrelenting, everything so frustrating, a whole new level of impatience.

The anger builds without warning, the anger that you could not be saved.

It is like a bull with its feet tied, while someone waves a red flag at it. The need to scream instead of speaking feels like a common theme, but society just cannot handle the screams of a grieving mother, so she hides away at home.

She wants to scream in a paddock where the birds flock to far away trees.

Anger, one of the many emotions worn by a grieving parent, a consistent feeling to reflect the messiness of grief.

Grief between the lines

Some days

Some days you will do more,

some days you will do less,

and some days not much at all.

That my dear is an incredible feat.

You are getting through the days
even if they are hideously rocky,
emotional, and catastrophically
painful, all you can do is get
through.

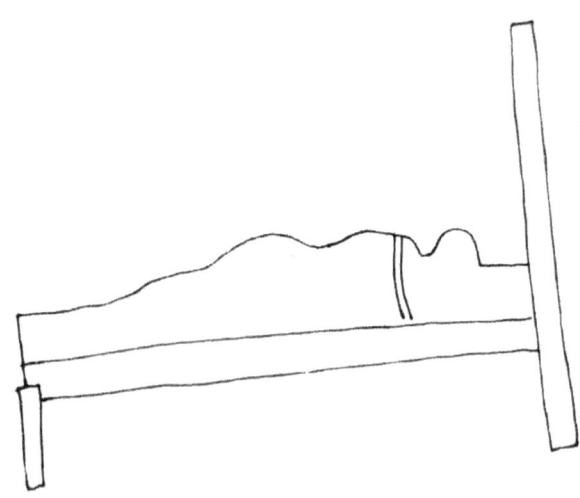

Emma Walker

Moments

People show up for a moment.

A fleeting moment to check in,

to chat things through.

A momentary shoulder,

or voice on the end of the telephone.

Sometimes you hang up the phone,

or get back into your car.

and wonder if they realize that every comfort is so momentary right now.

It is like you need to summon them back before the grief floodgates open.

Grief does not show up for a moment, it shows up for a lifetime.

The loneliness, the heartache,

the constant wind turbine of emotions.

Grief between the lines

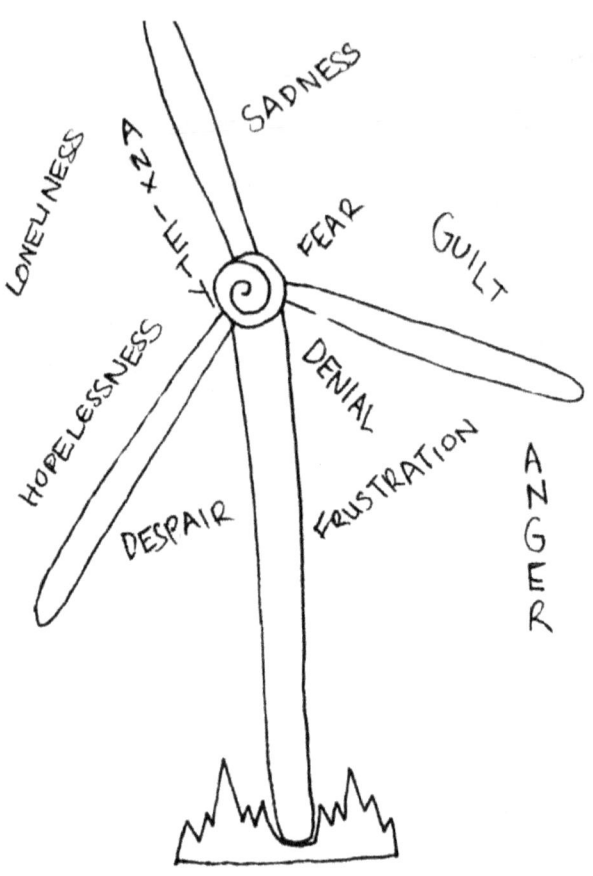

Emma Walker

Too sad for sunshine

Raindrops to match the tears.

Tear drops that reflect the realisation of every worst fear.

That bright light in the sky will never shine the same without you here beneath it.

Now I only welcome the rain, as it is the type of weather that reflects the pain.

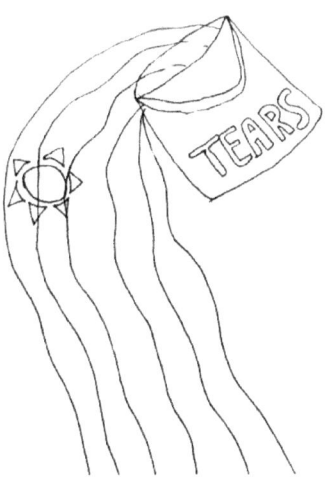

Grief between the lines

Help

You feel like you need help.

yet do not quite know what kind.

You think you ask for it and nobody

seems to hear you.

Maybe you are not making any sense,

but why does it feel like you have stamped your needs on your forehead.

Another day goes by, the help still not there.

Why cannot they hear me, it does not seem fair.

Then you realise it was always there.

It is inside you ready to be released.

For you are so much stronger than you think.

Emma Walker

Shadows

Sometimes grief makes you hide in the shadows of society, choosing the less populated places to lurk.

The supermarket aisles without trolleys and their borrowers.

The beaches where you can stare down at the sand or out into the ocean without bumping into someone.

The pavements where there is less traffic zooming past, less people out going about their day.

You wait for the day where you do not feel so avoidant of society, not knowing when and if it will come.

Grief between the lines

Safe places

You wrack your brain,

searching for safe places,

yet the list feels so small,

suffocatingly so.

Where is the reprieve,

where do grieving mothers go,

where are they safe from reminders.

Society has no such place,

or it feels that way anyway.

No safe place.

No place where the tear ducts can stand down for just a moment,

and the adrenaline levels settle, or where you can look up instead of down at your feet.

Society, thanks but no thanks, you do not offer what I need, a safe place to grieve.

Emma Walker

Not OK

Everyone around just going about
their day, sharing it to social
media, a place you readily avoid.

Here I am not going about anything,

I am not going about,

I am not going,

I am not,

OK.

I am not OK.

Grief between the lines

Eyes

Hyper-vigilant in grief,

weakened defence mechanisms,

reduced tolerance and capacity,

in need of comfort,

yet people around you do not know what to say.

You send a prompt only to be met with stark silence,

it feels like eyes watching you,

icebergs keeping you cold,

when you are really needing warmth.

Emma Walker

Hugs

Hold me, hug me,

try to find some words.

Some words of comfort,

words of belonging,

for that would help ease my mind.

I know there are no words that feel right,

but I appreciate your courage to say something despite.

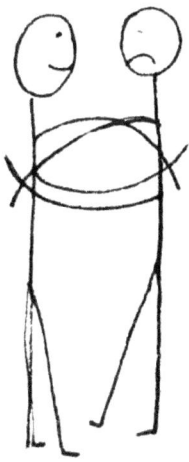

Grief between the lines

Slow Steps

Dewy grass, soggy leaves,

soft sand, gentle breeze.

Feeling blue, damp shoes,

disconnecting from society, from the triggers and the rush.

Long walks, solo steps,

one step at a time,

one walk at a time,

one day at a time.

Emma Walker

Floodgates

Tears flow like water gushing
through a dam that has been flooded
during a storm.

They continue to fill your eyes
each day, helping to release some
of this gut-wrenching pain. There
is an endless water supply from
your tear ducts, your body has
learnt to make sure that its
replenished knowing how much you
need to be able to cry to get
through each harrowing day.

Never ending tears for a never-
ending pain.

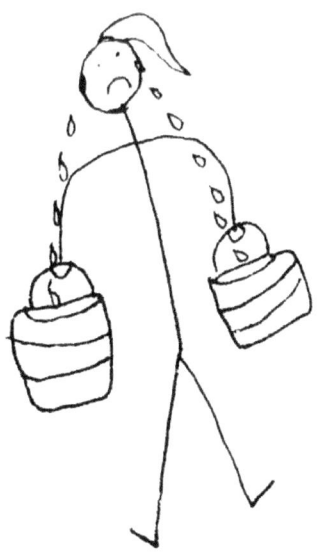

Grief between the lines

Tears

So many different types that you never knew existed before your eyes started producing them like an industrial factory. Theres tears that roll silently down your cheeks,

there are ones you can disguise in public with sunglasses,

there are loud distressed tears that come out anytime without warning, you try and give these tears space and privacy as they are sacred survival tears.

Emma Walker

Space

You want support but space,

like an astronaut needing their rocket.

The durable and adaptable kind of support that does not waver no matter how difficult and unpredictable the conditions.

Grief between the lines

Respect

Instead of beating yourself up on
the bad days, honour your survival
skills.

A lot of pain signifies a lot of
love for the person you have lost.

Emma Walker

Adrenaline

Always on edge, heart rate ready to spike at the drop of a hat.

Nowhere feels restful or calm,

nowhere to let my guard down.

The times I have tried have led me to a stressed-out state of mind.

In these times, if only all people were kind.

Peaceful places feel hard to find.

Grief between the lines

Shy

Suddenly shy, or at least feeling this way.

It has been like this since the day you got taken away, my darling.

Emma Walker

Solo

Something you all have in common,
grief.

Yet each journey so unique.

There is a common respect there for
each and every traveller on this
long and lonely journey.

An acknowledgment of their strength
as you must have for yours to keep
on going, day after day.

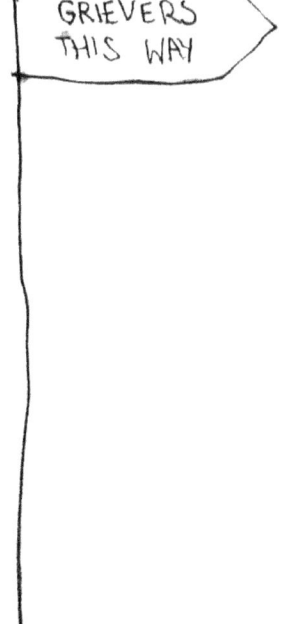

Grief between the lines

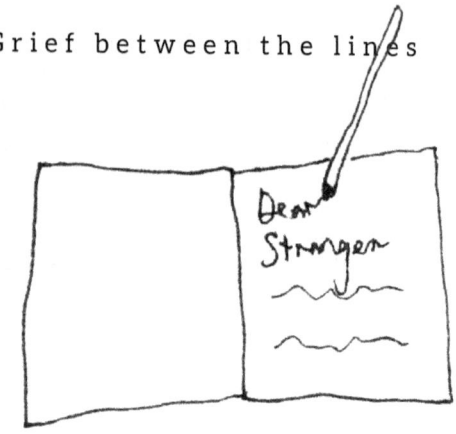

Dear stranger

I am jealous but it is not your fault.

I look at you and wonder why your loved one got to stay when mine did not.

Sometimes it feels as though this reality is shoved in my face, everywhere I turn.

Again, knowing it is not your fault.

If only for the next while, my eyes could filter out what is too painful for my heart and soul to see.

I am needing some reprieve.

Emma Walker

Distractions

Outdoors not indoors,

active not sedentary

the less pressure the better.

Craft over chores,

please do not ask for more.

Some things help, albeit
temporarily, and others not at all.

Some people help to ease while
others cause me to freeze.

I have tried many things, and most
have failed.

There are no distractions that
really help,

but it is quite OK to try different
things again and again.

Grief between the lines

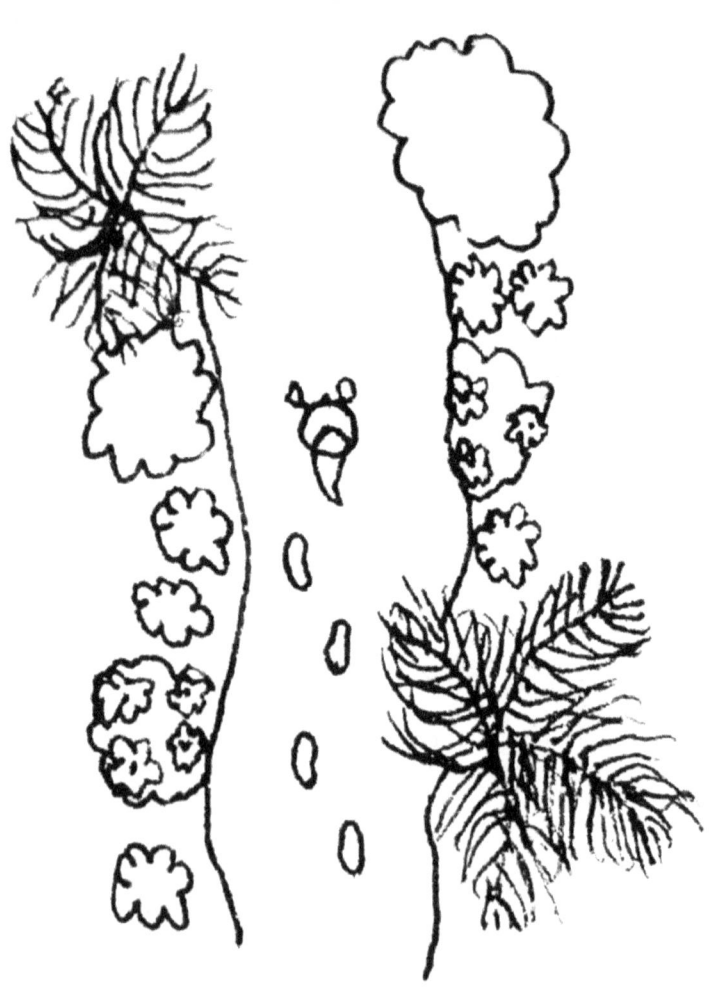

Emma Walker

Waves

Hours and hours,

walking alongside,

staring into,

gazing at,

listening to,

strolling near, headed for quiet ones, where nature drowns passerby conversations.

Soft sand, hard sand,

cold or not,

the beach and its ocean, currently stands as the most soothing spot.

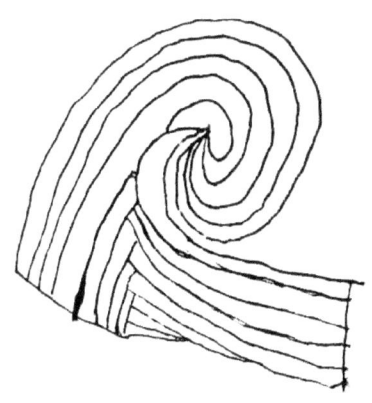

Grief between the lines

Awkward

If your grief makes people uncomfortable,

that is not your fault.

Do not try to bend, you are already broken.

Emma Walker

Patience

These days it feels patience is a thing of the past.

The fuse is short.

Capacity string always taught.

Existing at my limits.

Anything or everything can push past them like an impatient traveller at a train station.

No patience, no tolerance, ready to snap,

It is just not clear who or what it will be directed at.

Grief between the lines

Moon

You show up every night.

I sit and stare at you.

I do this quite a lot.

I am usually alone,

just you, me, and the ocean.

As I walk past houses in the street,

I do not hear a peep.

Everyone indoors,

perhaps some of them asleep.

 I sit and cry for my loved one,

tears sliding down my cheeks,

nobody can really see me,

your ocean reflection rather weak.

There is more privacy in the evening once you show up, your waxy presence in the sky allowing me the space to walk, sit and cry.

Emma Walker

Grief between the lines

Bubble wrap

I need to protect my heart,

my soul,

my mind,

I am hurting.

I need space.

Space from pressure,

space from the rat race.

Let me wrap myself

and do not try to tear it down,

I am wrapped up for a reason,

a very precious reason,

a reason you may know,

a person you may know,

with them is gone,

my heart and my soul.

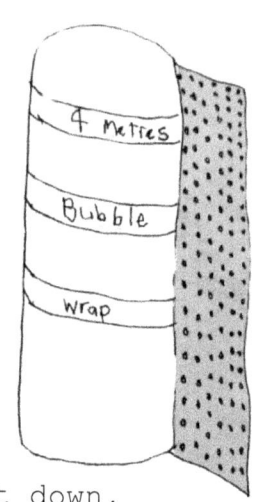

Emma Walker

See you later

It is OK to push them away,

if in your hardest moments,

they chose not to stay.

Let them shy away and "not know what to say".

You can try and remind them the silence only pushes you away, it does not "give you space".

Whatever you do, protect your heart, it is going through enough, its torn apart.

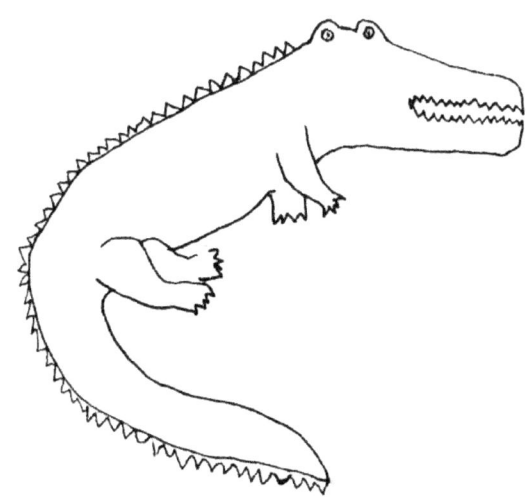

Grief between the lines

Feelings

I need to scream,

I need to shout,

I need to wail,

I need to howl.

Humans are restricted,

unlike animals at the zoo,

we do not get to scream and shout,

people will probably judge if we even pout.

If there was soundproofing in this house,

I would scream,

to let some feelings out.

Instead, my pillow is my soundproof space,

it sort of helps to ease the pain,

but there really is no great expressive space.

Emma Walker

Boundaries

Speak your truth,

only yours you know,

show respect,

but do not let your boundaries go.

All you can do is your best,

and remember to give your body plenty of rest.

Grief between the lines

Connections

Listening to music,

lyrics I never knew,

Now when I hear,

I think about you.

So much power,

so much meaning,

and so much connection,

to the memories of you.

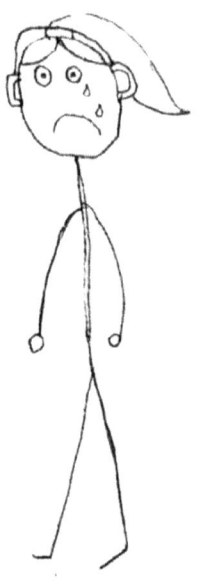

Emma Walker

Walking

I will walk in all weather,

I cannot stay inside.

All these feelings,

nowhere to hide.

Fresh air I need,

Cold breeze, yes please.

Blowing trees,

wind swept leaves.

Out in the open,

cold air on my face,

nowhere feels right,

my body in fight or flight.

I will be outside in all weather,

and I will be thinking of you,

my greatest treasure.

Grief between the lines

Bending

We are hurting,

and yet we are still bending,

to the rules of society,

to give space to the non-grievers going about their day.

To them we bite our tongues there is nothing we can say.

So much on our minds,

so much on our plates.

They are not to know,

but my gosh it is hard when you just want to run away.

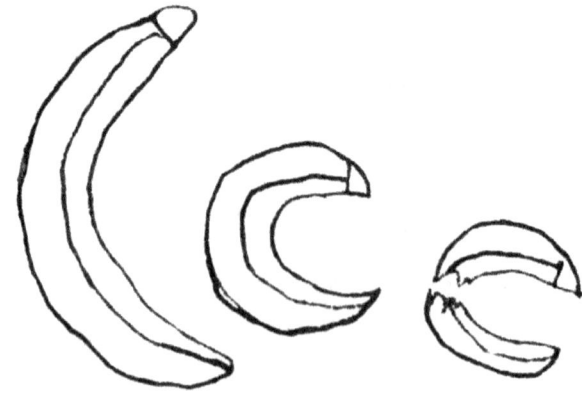

Emma Walker

Messages

It is so frustrating when your body bottles the feelings up, refusing to let them out.

You know there is no escaping the grief, the feelings will eventually come out.

It might be in a trickle, it might be in a flood, it can all come crashing down with such a thud.

Write the feelings down, even if they do not pour out your mouth.

Sometimes your mind is racing so far ahead, you need time to process to know what you need to let out.

Let your body do what it needs, it is perfectly understandable to feel tangled in the reeds.

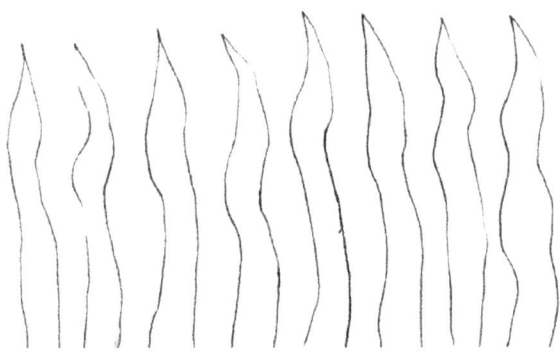

Grief between the lines

Loss and lost

Grief comes with loss,

loss of your loved one,

loss of the future you planned,

loss of your identity,

loss of purpose,

loss of smiles and laughter,

loss of meaning,

loss of your ability to show as much compassion and show up to those around you as much as you would like to.

Basically, when you lose someone who love more than anything in the world, you feel like you have lost everything.

That right there is why there is no time frame for grief, no right way to tackle it, there is no tackling it, it is with you every day, in every way.

It represents deep love, and with this loss comes deep pain.

Emma Walker

Appetite

Its either not there or
overzealous, nothing in balance,
nothing the same, body and mind
forever changed.

Grief between the lines

Nightmare

Nightmare after nightmare,

everywhere I go,

everywhere I look.

Waking up in the morning,

wondering how to do this,

how do I get up, shower, and start my day when all this pain shows no signs of shying away.

Emma Walker

TV

The light box on the wall,

no real use to me at all.

I once found it entertaining and now it serves no purpose at all.

Some find it distracting and others disagree.

It can be hard to concentrate, that we can all agree.

The brain fog is daily, we feel tired and slow, the effects of this grief, taking their toll.

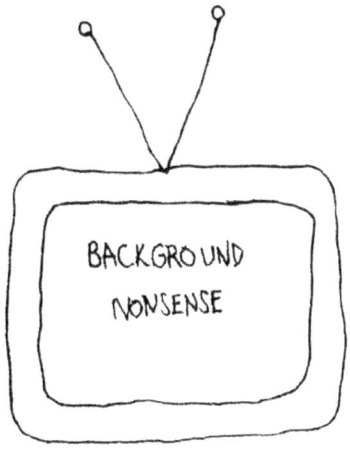

Grief between the lines

Ready to pounce

Anything can hurt,

no matter how small.

It takes all your energy to protect your heart and your soul.

It could be someone's words, or a lack thereof, it could be music, television, someone's road rage or an awkward encounter with a stranger.

Everything accumulates and when you start your day with an overflowing cup, there sure isn't much room to take on any of the above.

Emma Walker

Fatigue

Weary to your core,

yet not able to sleep.

Used to be a napper, but now cannot catch a wink.

Early morning wake ups, reality strikes,

evenings spent grieving,

both leaving me a mess.

Theres really no rest when your loved one is gone,

the grief is with you, all day and night long.

www.ingramcontent.com/pod-product-compliance
Lightning Source LLC
Chambersburg PA
CBHW070440010526
44118CB00014B/2132